DEDICATION

I would like to dedicate this storybook to a sweet and wonderful little girl who experienced some of Sweet Pea's adventures. You know who you are!

Also, to another sweet and wonderful young lady who encouraged me to write another child's book. You know who you are too!

ISBN: 978-1-387-47651-0

Published November 2022 by LuLu Publishing

THE

STORY

OF

SWEET PEA'S

ADVENTURES

SWEET PEA'S ADVENTURES

Sweet Pea lives with her mom, dad, big brother and sister. Her mom worked so grandma and grandpa watched Sweet Pea when she was very little.

Sweet Pea was very smart and learned quickly by watching everyone around her. Let's say Sweet pea learned too quickly. She wanted to experience everything she could.

At six months old she was busy buzzing around the house in a walker trying to get into everything she could. Grandma showed her a deck of cards to play and learn from. Sweet Pea quickly discovered where Grandma put the cards on the walker. Sweet Pea found them and pulled them out of the box and tossed them all over the floor. Finally Grandma learned ro put the cards in a place where Sweet Pea could not find them.

In December Sweet Pea found the Christmas tree that was very inviting. The lights that surrounded the tree were much too inviting to stay away from. She pulled and pulled the string of lights until she had them all tangled around herself. Luckily, Grandma came to her rescue before the tree came tumbling down around Sweet Pea and her walker. The tree came down early that Christmas.

Soon the time came when Sweet Pea did not need the walker any longer. The adventures got even more fun and dangerous for her. Sweet Pea didn't walk around, she ran. She could easily outrun Grandma and Grandpa. She learned to lock bedroom doors and locked herself inside the laundry room. Getting a chair she crawled up on the counter and found the tube of red paint that Grandma told her she could not have until she got older. Grandma's "no" usually did not mean "no!" She found a tube of red paint. She took off the lid and squeezed the tube leaving paint all over the room and herself. She finally unlocked the door when the tube of paint was empty. What a mess she left in the laundry room and all over herself.

Grandma and Sweet Pea decided to make some Christmas cookies. It was fun shaping the cookies into trees, Santas, and stockings. The first batch went into the oven and Sweet Pea loved the wonderful smell coming from the oven. She could not wait any longer. Sweet Pea opened the oven door and reached in to grab a cookie.

Sweet Pea loved music. She would convince Grandma and Grandpa to go with her into the music room and dance and dance even on the bed until both Grandma and Grandpa could stand no more. " Time , Sweet Pea, to sit down and play a game."

Grandpa loves decorating for birthdays. He would always hang balloons from the chandelier above the kitchen table. Sweet Pea wanted those balloons. Up on the chair and up on the table went Sweet Pea. She pulled down all the balloons and then started hanging on the chandelier. Back and forth went Sweet Pea until Grandpa grabbed her and got her down on the floor.

It was Christmas morning and Sweet Pea could not sleep a minute longer. She thought she heard Santa on the roof and she was excited to see if he brought her the scooter she wanted so much. She kept thinking of all the places she would ride her new scooter. It was electric and went wherever she wanted to go. There it was shiny bright red sitting under the Christmas tree. It was cold and snowy outside, but Sweet Pea was determined to ride her new scooter. She went down the steep driveway and up the road to show her friend her new scooter.

Grandma has a glass cabinet where she keeps all her special knick knacks. Sweet Pea couldn't figure out how to get in that thing to get those pretty glass horses. She thought if she could kick the glass she could get into the cabinet. Laying on the floor in front of the cabinet, Sweet Pea raised both feet and kicked hard. Crash went the glass.

Sweet Pea watched as her big brother went riding a four wheeler around the property. Sweet Pea wanted to ride too. When her brother went into the house, she climbed up on the four wheeler, turned the key and turned the handle just like her brother did. Off, zoomed the four wheeler straight for the tree ahead.

Next door to Sweet Pea is a farm. Everytime she would go in the car to visit Uncle Joe she would see a pretty black horse in the fenced yard. She wanted to pet that horse and climb the fence to get on his back. The next morning the sun shined brightly through her window and woke her up. Today is the best day ever to ride Blackie thought Sweet Pea. Getting dressed and grabbing Dusty her pet dog, they climbed out her bedroom window. Soon they were at Blackie's fence.

Blackie saw Sweet Pea and galloped toward her snorting his nose the whole way. Sweet Pea climbed over the wire fence and went toward Blackie. Suddenly, Blackie reared up and got ready to trample Sweet Pea. She was in trouble and Dusty knew it. He barked furiously and distracted Blackie from trampling Sweet Pea. Quickly, Sweet Pea felt danger and climbed back through the fence.

Sweet Pea was almost asleep when she remembered something. Her favorite doll was over at her friend's home. It was dark out, but Sweet Pea was sure she could find her friend's house to pick up her doll. Putting on her coat, Sweet Pea quietly stepped to the front door. Uh, oh it was locked. That's okay she thought, I will get a kitchen chair to unlock the door. Down the front steps and up the sidewalk went Sweet Pea. It was getting darker and Sweet Pea got turned around and lost her way.

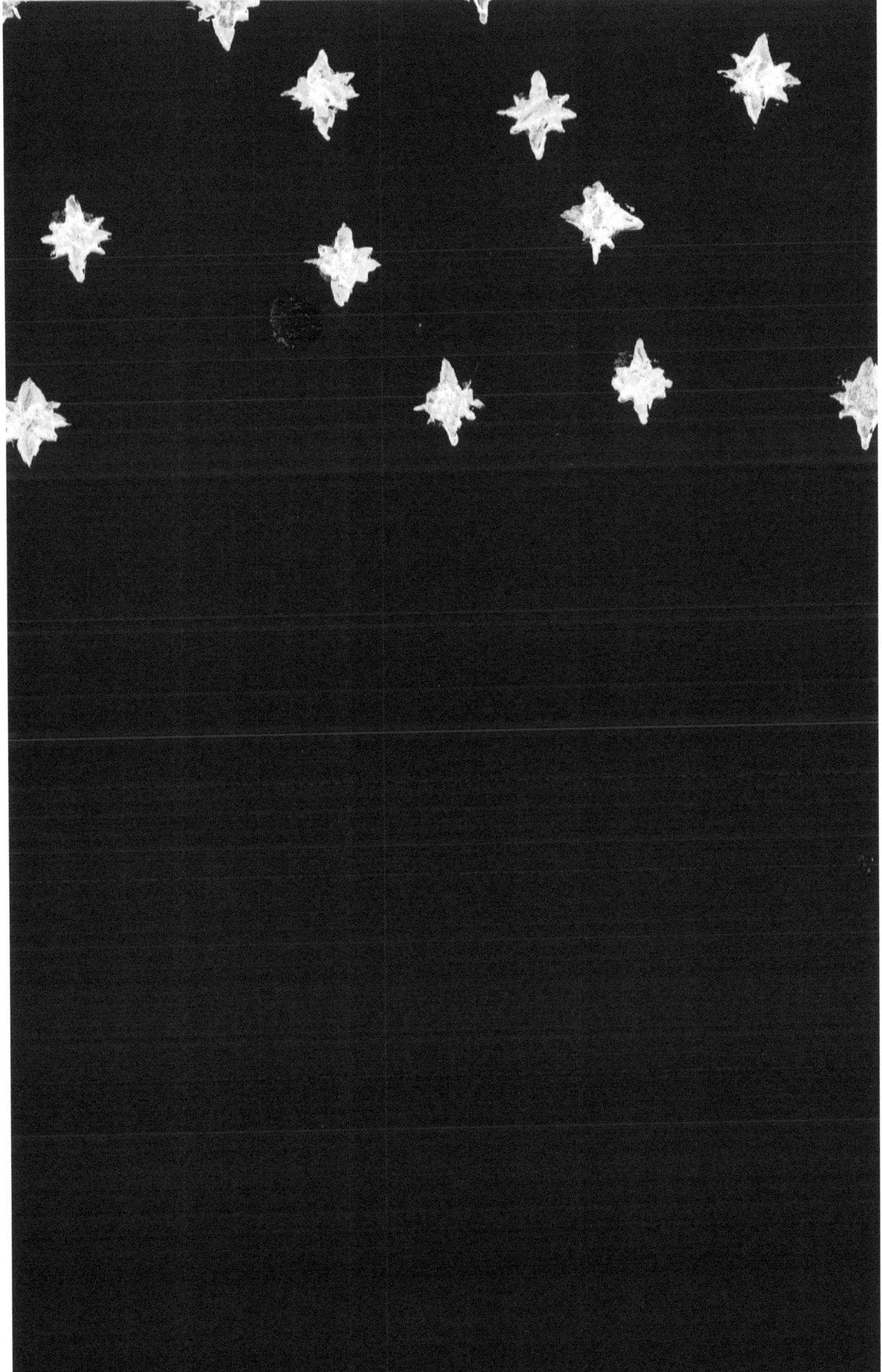

We can all learn from Sweet Pea's adventure. Some things can cause us serious injury. Can electricity hurt you from electrical cords?

What's wrong with sticking your hand in a hot oven?

What would happen if you got stuck in a lock door?

Is tasting paint ok?

Could you get hurt jumping on a bed?

What could happen if you hung on a chandelier?

What could happen to Sweet Pea riding a scooter down a steep driveway and then down a road?

What might happen if you kicked glass out of a cabinet?

What could have happened to Sweet Pea on the four wheeler?

Are all horses friendly?

Why should we ask for help before we go somewhere by ourselves?

Sweet Pea learned some valuable lessons.

THE

END